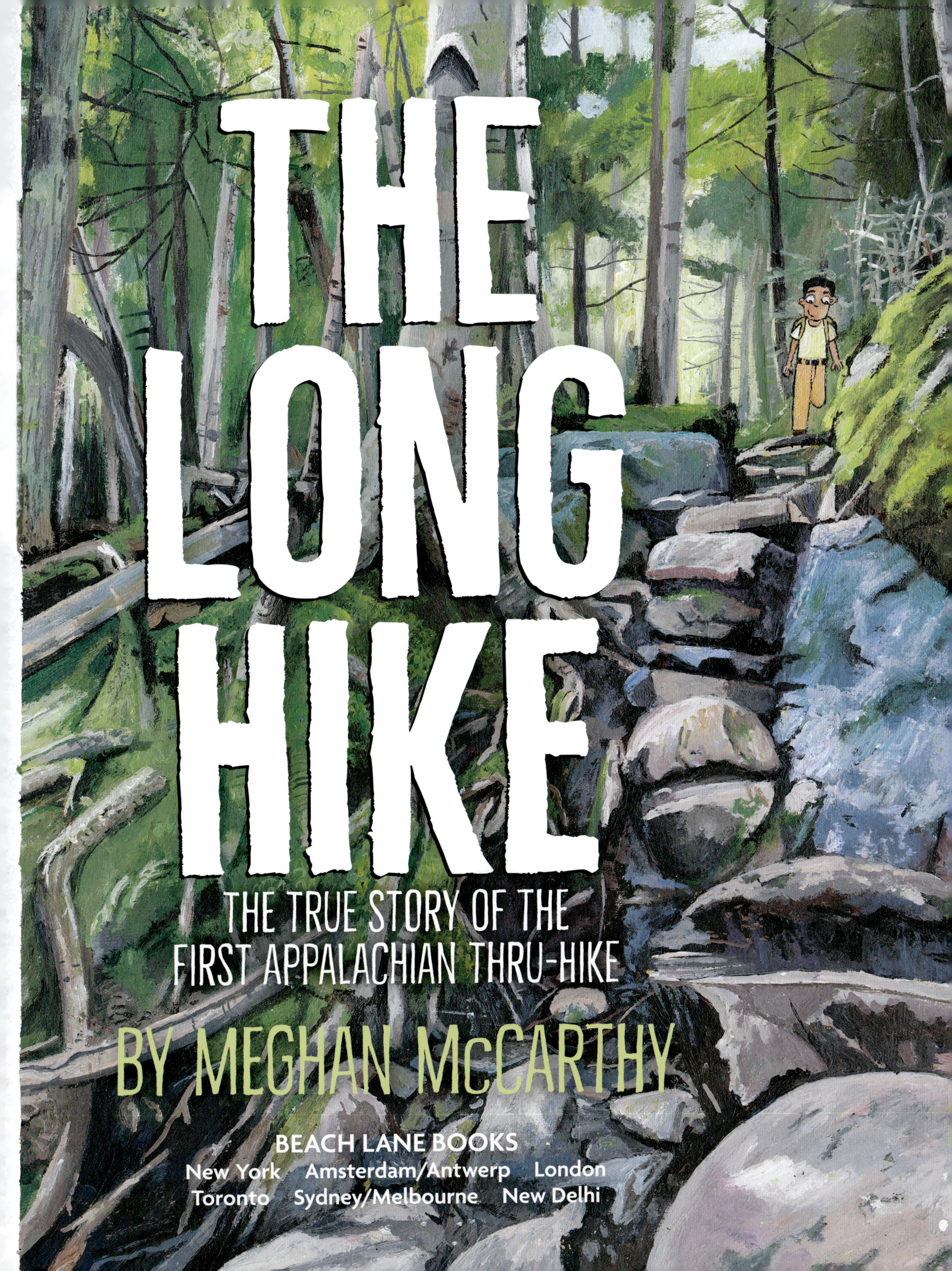

THE LONG HIKE

THE TRUE STORY OF THE FIRST APPALACHIAN THRU-HIKE

BY MEGHAN McCARTHY

BEACH LANE BOOKS
New York Amsterdam/Antwerp London
Toronto Sydney/Melbourne New Delhi

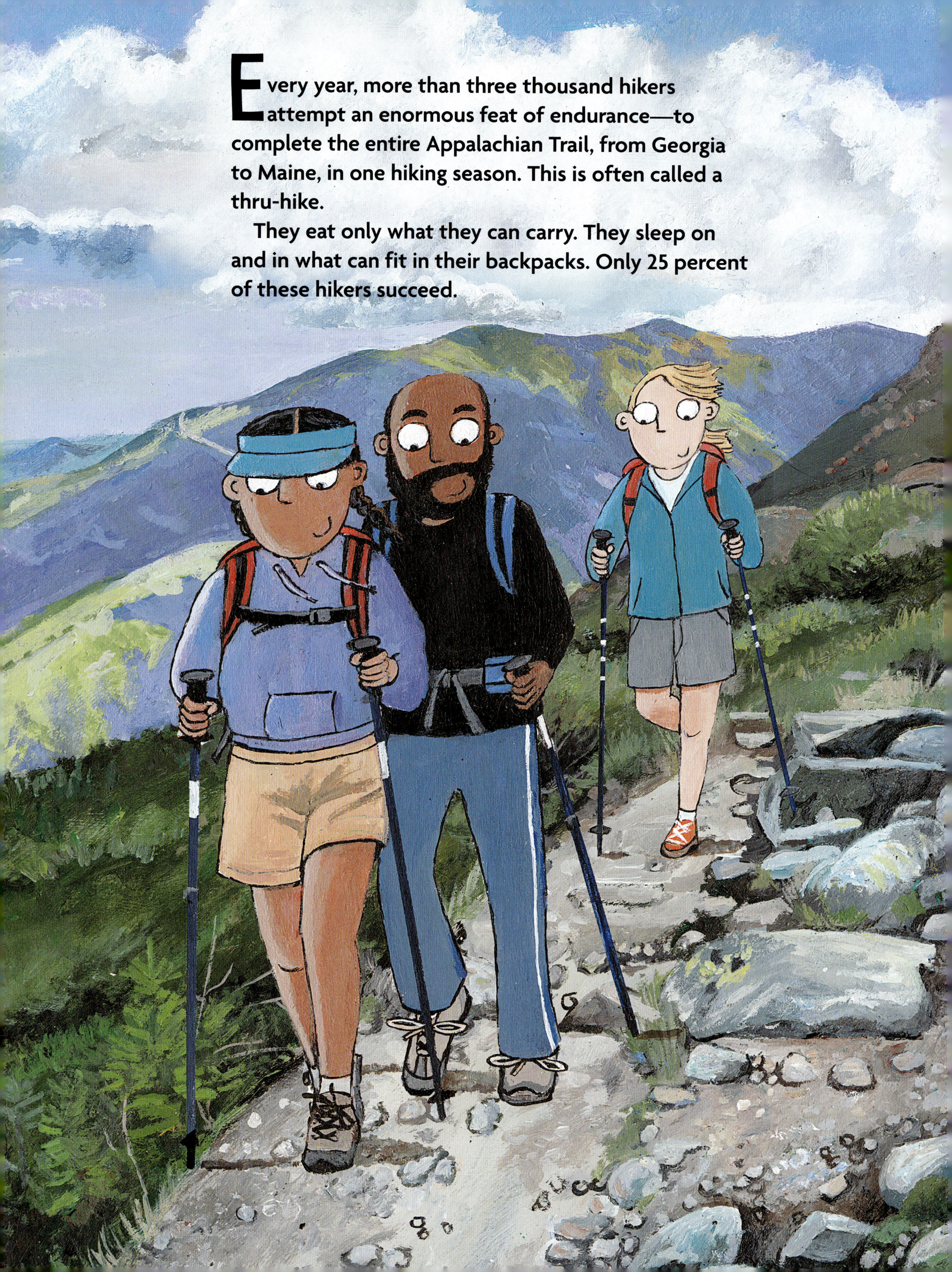

Every year, more than three thousand hikers attempt an enormous feat of endurance—to complete the entire Appalachian Trail, from Georgia to Maine, in one hiking season. This is often called a thru-hike.

They eat only what they can carry. They sleep on and in what can fit in their backpacks. Only 25 percent of these hikers succeed.

The desire to thru-hike the Appalachian Trail was dreamed up by this guy: Earl Shaffer. Earl was sent to the Pacific as a soldier during World War II. In his free time, he wrote poetry that reflected the sadness of war:

Earl Shaffer in his uniform

No single building stood unharmed
And most were heaps of trash,
Reminded me of forest
Stripped of all but stumps and slash.

The war in the Pacific ended on September 2, 1945. Earl traveled back home to the United States. He wrote a poem to reflect the end of his wartime service:

There are friendships we all cherish
That the home folks cannot know
There will come the restless longing
To always be on the go.

After Earl's return home, he made plans to be "on the go" once more. Prior to the war, Earl had planned to hike the Appalachian Trail with his best friend, Walter. Sadly, Walter died while fighting for his country. "Iwo Jima was the end of life's trail for him, leaving me to travel alone," Earl said. He was "confused and depressed" and decided to "walk the war out of my system." He wanted to replace the darkness of war with the calming and restorative embrace of nature.

Earl's motto was "carry as little as possible but choose that little with care." He took his "little black book" to jot down his experiences as he went, as well as color film to use in his camera. He packed a week's worth of food (which he would replenish as he went), a pot to cook in, and a few shirts and pants to wear. He also took the following:

Marine Corps poncho
(also used as a tarp)
Prewar Kodak Retina
Wool socks
Sewing kit
Marble Company
match safe
Bird shooter
boots

Earl ordered trail maps, but they never arrived. He daringly ventured out without them. His backpack was "bulky and heavy." On April 4, 1948, the hike began in Georgia.

From Earl's little black book:
Got cold and blustery toward morning and I hated like poison to get up . . . Took pics of flower trees. Saw a wild turkey.

During WWII, many volunteers who maintained the trail were shipped off to fight in the war. While they were away, vines rapidly grew and storms caused trees to fall, covering the trail. The trail's blazes (white marks on trees to help guide hikers) faded away. Earl wrote that "the famous footpath seemed on the way to oblivion."
April 6th.
Two days on the trail.
Walked nearly ten miles before learning I was off trail . . . had to walk back.

In about two weeks, Earl reached North Carolina. Wherever the trail passed a town, Earl stopped to buy more supplies. He bought food like canned Vienna sausages, oatmeal, and potatoes. Can you imagine carrying those heavy foods on your back?

Weather foggy. trail hard to find . . . Getting dark. Had feeling of the power of nature.

Soon Earl's markings of days and times in his little black book all but disappeared. Blisters appeared on Earl's feet. "Hiking became an exquisite kind of torture," he later wrote. Earl came up with an unusual solution to this problem: "to put sand in my boots and wear no socks until my feet toughened."

Looked like rain which came in night outening fire.
Spent morning trying to dry clothes. Wood so damp.

Earl was nearing the first month of his thru-hike on the Appalachian Trail, where it crisscrosses North Carolina and Tennessee.

Thinking of Walter
and composing poems.

Earl crossed into Virginia at
the beginning of May.
Sun. May 2
Saw two black snakes
both seven or 8 ft long.
Took pictures of first.

Although Earl tried to remain solitary, he still had many encounters with people and enjoyed them. He wrote about one such encounter:

Had only gone about a mile when a gov. car stopped and a fella asked if I wanted a ride. Refused as usual. He then asked if I'd talk a while. He pulled over and we had a long gabfest. He was Bill Lord, Park Ranger stationed in Floyd, VA . . . We discussed photography, flowers and just about everything else. He invited me to his place if I get thru there again. Swell guy.

As Earl snaked through Virginia, West Virginia, and back to Virginia, the leaves on the trees fully opened, and fruiting plants provided a welcome snack.

. . . dawdled at strawberry patches.

May 18th
Sang Lullaby Yodel as I hiked.
My voice must terrify wild things.

Earl crossed through Maryland but didn't make much mention of it in his little black book. Instead, he made a lot of notes about his home state of Pennsylvania.

Tues June 8
Am in no hurry to start because of wet brush. I had picked about a pint of wild strawberries along the way and I made cornbread to eat them with, downing shortcake style

. . . took pic of Lehigh Valley showing Allentown in far distance. Also pic showing valley farmland of rolling hills and woodland as far as the eye can see merging in the horizon over New Jersey.

Saw several deer.

By mid-June, Earl reached New Jersey. This was the state he disliked most, because New Jersey did not allow campfires. Though it was late spring and the days were warm, the temperatures still dropped to 40 degrees on some nights. Earl had no fire to keep him warm.

In about another week, Earl reached New York.
Sure am glad to be out of N.J. That no-fire law has me on the verge of pneumonia & Starvation.

Just as soon as Earl was out of New Jersey, he encountered a particularly crafty critter.

I heard it . . .

drinking from kettle of water I had ready for breakfast . . .

It licked my fry pan . . .

then began tearing apart box of spaghetti someone had left.

About two weeks later, Earl passed through Connecticut. Hiking through the spring and into the early summer had its issues:
mosquitoes very annoying.
. . . crossed area of heavy hemlock timber, hummocks, natural rock gardens, caverns, etc. Called Dark Forest.

Earl hiked through Massachusetts and into Vermont. Like all thru-hikers, Earl cooled off and got clean whenever he spotted the right opportunity.

Took brief swim.

By July, Earl was in New Hampshire. He climbed over Mount Washington, which has the most extreme weather in the country. The mountain claims several lives each year. In 2023, a new low was recorded on the summit, with a temperature of -46.9 degrees and a wind chill of -108.4.

It took Earl several weeks to hike through New Hampshire. One more state to go! Earl had been hiking for more than three months.

Crossed Me-NH line at 2:15 PM. 20th July.

Finally, Earl ventured into Maine, which contains some of the most desolate and wild parts of the trail. Multiple river crossings were required and still are to this day.

By the time Earl made it out of Maine's wilderness to a campground lean-to, word had gotten out. "Are you the man walkin' the trail?" asked a park ranger. The ranger said that reporters were looking for him. At ranger headquarters, Earl's picture was taken and he was interviewed, though the reporters promised to keep the news a secret until Earl finished his final mountain climb.

Earl finally arrived at his last challenge: Mount Katahdin. He finished in a leisurely fashion.

The Long Cruise was finished. Already it seemed like a vivid dream, through sunshine, shadow, and rain – Already I knew that many times I would want to be back again . . .

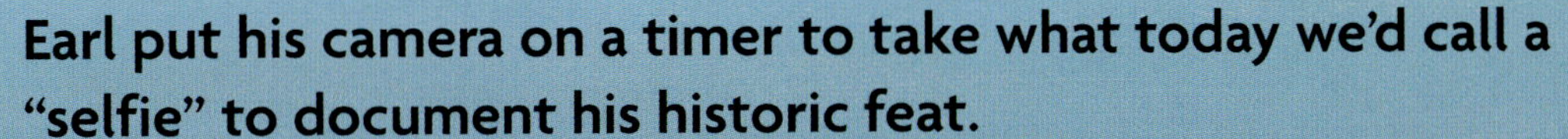

Earl put his camera on a timer to take what today we'd call a "selfie" to document his historic feat.

August 6, 1948, *The Baltimore Sun*:

The Appalachian Trail is 'conquered' at last!

Earl spent the rest of his years advocating to preserve his favorite hiking trail. At the age of forty-seven, he did indeed "go back again." Then, when he was nearly eighty, Earl hiked the Appalachian Trail one final time. It was on this last hike that he struggled.

1998 trail notebook:
Rock, rock, rock, and more rocks . . . nasty fall
Could have been disastrous bruises and contusions
The chief concern is getting thru unharmed

Unlike Earl's solo trip of '48, this time his brothers, sister, nieces, nephews, and fans helped by bringing food and water along the way. Despite his struggles, Earl broke another record, at that time being the oldest Appalachian thru-hiker. Newspapers reported his latest feat. Earl was also interviewed for *CBS This Morning*.

The flowers bloom, the songbirds sing,
And through it sun or rain,
I walk the mountain tops with spring
From Georgia north to Maine.

AUTHOR'S NOTE

Once the pandemic hit, I felt a burning desire to exit New York City and commune with nature. I needed a new book topic, and one about the Appalachian Trail seemed right. This is when I stumbled upon the story of Earl Shaffer. I was fascinated by the fact that Earl served in World War II. My grandfather was in the navy then, though he rarely talked about it and was depressed after the war, just as Earl seemed to be. Earl's brother John described Earl as "stubborn and tenacious." I think it takes those qualities to not only hike the entire Appalachian Trail (AT) in one go, but to also get the publicity required to designate oneself as "the first thru-hiker."

View from Mt. Jefferson and Mt. Clay

I loved Earl's little quirks, such as his penchant for sockless travel. Of course, after he hiked all of those miles sockless, his boots developed a pungent scent and remain that way to this day. "They are smelly," said one curator at the National Museum of American History. "Those cabinets are opened as little as possible." Earl also traveled with one change of clothes on his last hike. To keep somewhat clean, he would "find a stream, try to stay halfway civilized."

Earl's life was a simple one. For much of his life, he lived on a small homestead without running water, a refrigerator, a phone, or electricity. His home sat next to a meadow that kept his goats fed and happy, as well as a stream where berries grew along its bank. Earl enjoyed picking the berries and leaving them, along with other "garden goodies," as a friend remembers, on neighbors' doorsteps. He was an antiques dealer, tinkered with Volkswagen buses, played folk tunes on his guitar, and wrote poetry.

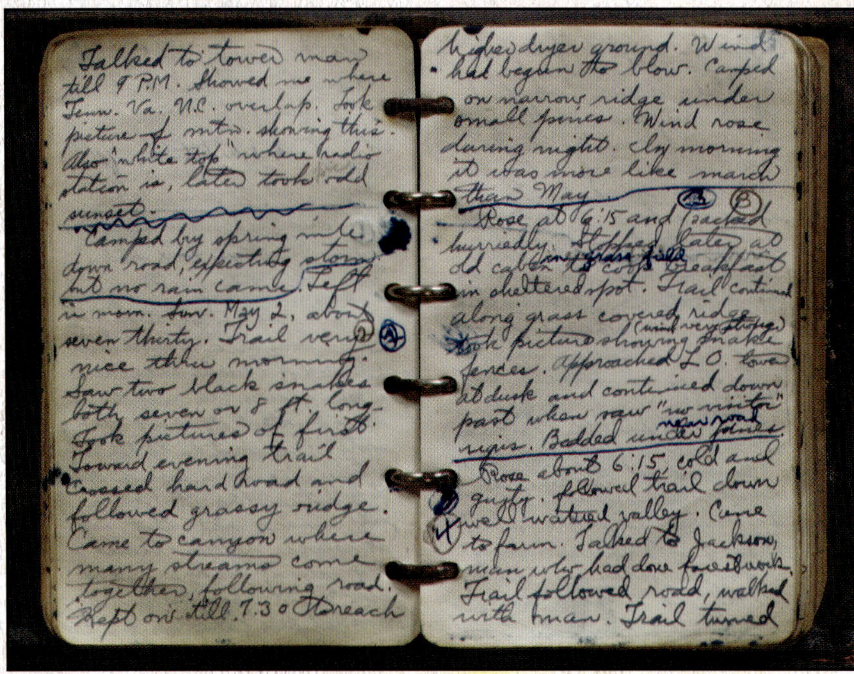

Talked to tower man
till 9 P.M. Showed me where
Tenn. Va. N.C. overlap. Took
picture of mts. showing this.
Also "white top" where radio
station is, later took old
sunset.
Camped by spring mile
down road, expecting storm
but no rain came. Left
in morn. [illegible] May 2, about
seven thirty. Trail very
nice thru morning.
Saw two black snakes
both seven or 8 ft. long.
Took pictures of first.
Toward evening trail
crossed hard road and
followed grassy ridge.
Came to canyon where
many streams come
together, following road.
Kept on till 7:30 to reach

higher drier ground. Wind
had begun to blow. Camped
on narrow ridge under
small pines. Wind rose
during night. By morning
it was more like March
than May.
Rose at 6:15 and packed
hurriedly. Stopped later at
old cabin [illegible] breakfast
in sheltered spot. Trail continued
along grass covered ridge
(wind very strong)
took picture showing snake
fences. Approached L.O. tower
at dusk and continued down
past when saw "no visitor"
signs. Bedded under pines.
Rose about 6:15, cold and
gusty, followed trail down
well watered valley. Came
to farm. Talked to Jackson,
man who had done forest work.
Trail followed road, walked
with man. Trail turned

Earl's little black book

During Earl's last AT hike, when he was seventy-nine, he complained that the trail had become more of a rigorous hike. In 1968, the land became federally protected, so portions of the trail were moved to go up mountain ridges for better views and to avoid roads and towns wherever possible. The AT eventually became over 158 miles longer. Shaffer remarked that the trail's relocation, making it subsequently more difficult to traverse, "missed the point." Earl added, "They call it a scenic trail, but you don't see a lot of scenery because you're staring at your feet the whole way because of rocks." Many younger hikers would disagree, however, seeing the boulders and "scrambling" as a fun challenge.

Newspapers describe Earl as a "folk hero," and one said that he had a "cultlike following." Despite this, he seemed quite humble and spoke in a drawl. "I just like to walk in the woods and sleep on mountaintops," he said. "I haven't done anything anyone else couldn't do." Earl gave himself the trail name "The Crazy One," possibly for good reason. On his last hike, he refused to modernize his hiking equipment. He lugged around another WWII backpack that one journalist said "looks like it should be in a museum," but then added, "It fits him just fine." Though Earl struggled on his 1998 hike, he amazingly finished without anything serious happening. *The Philadelphia Inquirer* described a snapshot of Earl's day:

> **He peeled off his 40-pound pack, gobbled four hard-boiled eggs and a package of 20 crackers, spooning jelly on each one or directly into his mouth. He unrolled his bedroll on the wooden floor and slept for three hours with his boots on.**

When Earl was asked if he'd hike the trail again, he said, "Ab-so-lute-ly not . . . It's the fiftieth anniversary, and I couldn't stay home. I had to."

Earl passed away from cancer, with his friends and family by his side, at the age of eighty-three. The Earl Shaffer Foundation was founded the year of his death, to continue his legacy. You can read more about Earl at earlshaffer.com.

THE TRAIL TODAY
(Twenty-First Century)

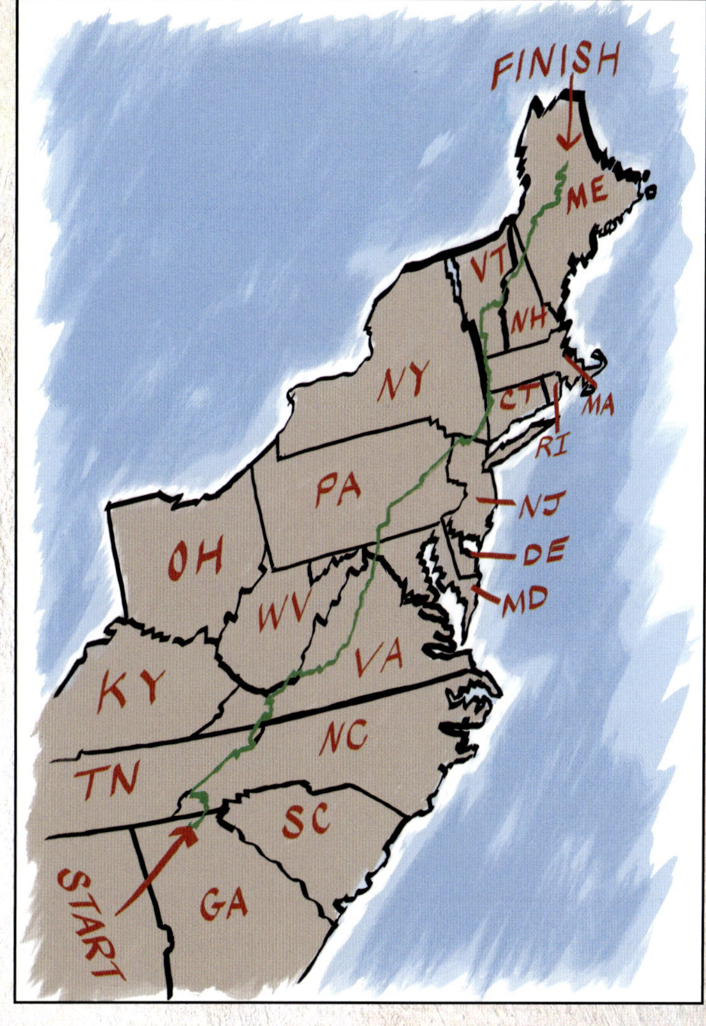

I've been aware of the Appalachian Trail since my dad section hiked the last 100 Miles in Maine, right around the time of Earl's last hike. It was a big deal because back then, cell phones weren't common, and there was no easy way for him to get help once entering the hundred miles. My dad said that at the time, the region was not only remote but depleted of modern civilization's trappings. The area had no electricity in keeping with Baxter State Park's namesake, who wanted the area to remain "forever wild." My dad describes his hike as "tense" because it was so remote. He returned from his journey with stories of thru-hikers who wouldn't let anything stop them from completing their trek. He stumbled upon an older woman whose face was entirely black and blue. She'd fallen on rocks but refused to relent to the pain. So she went to the ER, got her broken nose splinted, and then returned to the trail. Her face was harmed but not her spirit.

In the twenty years since both Earl's last hike and my dad's, equipment has gotten lighter and more advanced. Many hikers also now carry SOS emergency alert devices. Aside from more modernized equipment, little else has changed. By the time I got my contract for the Shaffer book, I'd been hiking bits and pieces of the AT wherever possible, to document it. When I was doing a school visit in West Virginia, I rented a car and took a detour on the way back to the DC airport. I drove to a beautiful part of Virginia that contained rolling green hills, sprinkled with farms. I got in a nice four-mile hike on the AT, which is, as many parts of the trail are, entirely plastered in rocks. While I was hiking at a good pace, a guy flew by me, all while carrying a huge backpack that looked at least fifty pounds. He stopped ahead of me, so when I caught up, we chatted a bit about the shoes hikers wear and even the knee injuries many have. Accompanying the hiker

Twister at Virginia/West Virginia line

was a small dog, who also had her own backpack. As with all people who thru-hike the AT, this guy had a trail name, which was "Chowder." His dog had a trail name too. "Twister," he explained, "likes to go in circles." His little dog carried her own food—about three days' worth at a time.

Fast-forward to this summer, when I was doing a seven-mile hike on another portion of the AT, this time in New York. The sun was setting, and I had to get back to the car in time, before the woods enveloped me in complete darkness. I was flagged down by an older woman, who told me that she had just turned eighty. I said, "Wow, you don't look it!" She told me that her knees were bothering her, but she was determined to trek on. She was looking for a water source. I told her that the only one I'd passed had turned into a muddy hole due to a lack of rainfall. Her trail name was "Grambo"—a combination of "Grandma" and "Rambo." Her grandkids liked to check in on her progress. Instead of hiking the whole AT in one go, she was doing sections at a time, flying home, then flying back to her last end point and resuming—a retirement hobby of sorts.

One of the biggest changes to the Appalachian Trail since Earl's first hike in '48 is the social aspect. There is a greater chance of encountering and even becoming best friends with fellow thru-hikers. The difference between the lone thru-hiker and one who eventually finds a group to hike with seems stark. The lone hike is a cerebral experience. I listened to one lone hiker talk about how emotional his lone hike was—that his brain had cycled through every past trauma he'd endured. His hike was a form of therapy. Those who hike in groups experience a community feel, and their hiking group becomes their "tramily."

Whether you are hiking alone or in a group, it takes a lot of mental strength to endure the endless rocks, the rain, the mud, the blisters, and the foot rot. Why people hike varies. Some just want the physical challenge, while others are trying to grapple with something gnawing at them. What Earl provided all of us is a gift for anyone seeking adventure—a unique and life-changing challenge.

View from Mt. Adams

TRAIL LINGO

Thru-hike: To hike the entire trail either southbound or northbound while only taking a day or two off here and there.

Zero day: To take a day off from hiking to recuperate, wash laundry, take a shower, and eat real food (sometimes).

On trail: Getting back on the trail and resuming the hike.

Trail magic: Food or drink, such as chips or soda, left free of charge for hikers to grab.

Trail angel: A person who leaves trail magic, helps hikers get to town and back, or allows hikers to stay in their house for free.

Blaze: A painted marker on trees and rocks to point hikers in the right direction to help them stay on trail.

White blaze: The AT uses white markings to direct hikers.

Tramily: "Trail family"—friends a hiker meets on the trail who become as close as family.

LNT (leave no trace): Not leaving wrappers, bottles, or even toilet paper behind on the trail.

Cairn: A stack of rocks to indicate which way to follow the trail, usually found above the tree line.

NOBO: Northbound hiking the AT—this is the traditional way to hike, as this is the way Earl first did it (from south, starting in Georgia, to north, ending in Maine).

SOBO: Southbound hiking the AT—from north, starting in Maine, to south, ending in Georgia.

Section hiker: A person who hikes sections of the AT.

Half-gallon ice-cream challenge: Around the halfway point, at Pine Grove Furnace State Park, hikers are offered the challenge of eating a half gallon of ice cream. It can give them an upset stomach, but many think that's worth the risk.

SELECT BIBLIOGRAPHY

Visit meghan-mccarthy.com for additional sources.

WEBSITES

appalachiantrail.org

earlshaffer.com

BOOKS

Donaldson, David and Maurice J. Forrester. *A Grip on the Mane of Life: An Authorized Biography of Earl V. Shaffer*. Appalachian Trail Museum, 2014.

Shaffer, Earl. *Before I Walked With Spring: The Doughboy Odyssey and Other Poems of World War II*. Earl Shaffer Foundation, 2008.

Shaffer, Earl. *Walking With Spring*. Appalachian Trail Conference, 1983.

RADIO

Wertheimer, Linda, host. *All Things Considered,* podcast, "Appalachian Hiker." October 22, 1998. https://www.npr.org/1998/10/22/1033340/appalachian-hiker.

EARL'S DIARIES—SMITHSONIAN

"Earl Shaffer's Appalachian Trail Hike Diary," 1948, Smithsonian, accessed July 2022–June 2025. https://transcription.si.edu/project/6734.

"The Long Cruise, 50th Anniversary AT hike, trail diary, book 1, 1998," Smithsonian, accessed August 2023. https://edan.si.edu/slideshow/viewer/?eadrefid=NMAH.AC.0828_ref108.

AUDIOVISUAL

Shaffer, John. *A Pictorial View of the Life of Earl Victor. Shaffer.* Video, 36 min. https://www.earlshaffer.com/video-downloads.

ARTICLES

"The Appalachian Trail is 'Conquered' At Last!" *The Baltimore Sun*, August 8, 1948.

Birnbaum, Stephen. "Grab Your Backpack, It's Time to Take a Hike." *Chicago Tribune*, August 10, 1986.

Bodani, Frank. "The Trail Blazer Makes a Second Attempt." *York Sunday News*, July 19, 1998.

Brown, Jennifer. "Happy Trail." *South Florida Sun Sentinel*, August 3, 1998.

Chase, Mrs. Dean. "Hiker, 29, Who Completed 2,000 Miles of Appalachian Trail Thinks Maine 'Swell.'" *Bangor Daily News*, August 6, 1948.

Ecenbarger, William. "Nature Finally Wins One." *The Philadelphia Inquirer*, July 15, 1984.

Hopey, Don. "Legendary Love for the Trail." *Pittsburgh Post Gazette*, July 2, 1995.

Hymon, Steve. "Earl V. Shaffer, 83; First to Walk Entire Length of Appalachian Trail." *Los Angeles Times*, May 26, 2002.

Johnson, Lizzie. "He lost his best friend in WWII. A trailblazing hike helped him heal." *Washington Post*, July 27, 2023.

King, Brian. "'The Long Cruise' of Earl Shaffer." Appalachian Trail Conservancy, August 4, 2023. appalachiantrail.org/official-blog/the-long-cruise-earl-shaffer-at-thru-hike/.

Marshall. "The Story Is in the Pictures." The Trek, October 14, 2019. https://thetrek.co/appalachian-trail/the-story-is-in-the-pictures/.

Martin, Douglas. "Earl Shaffer, First to Hike Length of Appalachian Trail in Both Directions, Dies at 83." *The New York Times*, May 12, 2002.

"No More Electricity, Toilets or Hot Baths In Baxter State Park." *The New York Times*, December 20, 1987.

"Pa. Man Starts to Hike to Top of Mount Katahdin." *Biddeford-Saco Journal*, August 5, 1948.

Pitts, Amanda and T. J. Del Santo. "Mt. Washington Records Coldest Wind Chill in U.S. History." WPRI.com, February 3, 2023. https://wpri.com/weather/winter-weather/mt-washington-records-coldest-wind-chill-in-u-s-history/.

Sharp, David. "No Worse for the Wear." *Hazleton Standard Speaker*, November 1, 1998.

Tucker, Abigail. "The Army Veteran Who Became the First to Hike the Entire Appalachian Trail." *Smithsonian Magazine*, July 2017.

Vitez, Michael. "Pioneer 79 And Climbing." *The Philadelphia Inquirer*, July 14, 1998.

Frost's Bolete or Candy Apple Bolete

Cairn

Goldenrod

ART NOTE

The more digital children's book art becomes, the more I want to do the opposite. The acrylic paintings for this book have been based almost entirely on my own photographs from hiking different portions of the AT.

For my dad, trail name "Psycho Bluesman"—your adventurous spirit is contagious.

Thanks to the Shaffer Foundation for help with this book.

BEACH LANE BOOKS
An imprint of Simon & Schuster Children's Publishing Division
1230 Avenue of the Americas, New York, New York 10020

Earl Schaffer's little black book and poetry excerpt permissions provided by The Shaffer Foundation
Earl Schaffer's Little Black Book Photograph provided by Earl Shaffer Papers,
Archives Center, National Museum of American History, Smithsonian Institution

Book design by Chloë Foglia and Meghan McCarthy

The text for this book was set in Agenda. The illustrations for this book were rendered in acrylic paint.
Manufactured in China
0226 SCP
First Edition
2 4 6 8 10 9 7 5 3 1
CIP data for this book is available from the Library of Congress.
ISBN 9781665949941
ISBN 9781665949958 (ebook)

Eastern Daisy Fleabane

Honey Fungus